Caring for Your
Iguana

Elizabeth Simon

Weigl Publishers Inc.

Project Coordinator
Heather C. Hudak

Design and Layout
Warren Clark
Bryan Pezzi

Copy Editor
Janice L. Redlin

Photo Research
Barbara Hoffman

Locate the iguana paw prints throughout the book to find useful tips on caring for your pet.

Published by Weigl Publishers Inc.
350 5th Avenue, Suite 3304, PMB 6G
New York, NY 10118-0069 USA
Web site: www.weigl.com

Library of Congress Cataloging-in-Publication Data

Simon, Elizabeth, 1976-
  Caring for your iguana / Elizabeth Simon.
      p. cm. -- (Caring for your pet)
  ISBN 1-59036-215-2 (softcover) 1-59036-195-4 (library bound : alk. paper)
  1. Iguanas as pets--Juvenile literature. I. Title. II. Caring for your pet (Mankato, Minn.)
  SF459.I38S56 2004
  639.3'9542--dc22

                              2004001002

                    Printed in the United States of America
                    1 2 3 4 5 6 7 8 9 0   08 07 06 05 04

Photograph and Text Credits
Every reasonable effort has been made to trace ownership and to obtain permission to reprint copyright material. The publishers would be pleased to have any errors or omissions brought to their attention so that they may be corrected in subsequent printings.

Cover: young green iguana on haliconia (©Brian Kenney); **Gerry Bucsis and Barbara Somerville:** pages 12, 14, 15, 16, 18/19, 20, 21, 23, 24, 26; **Diane Calkins/Click the Photo Connection:** page 4; **Corel Corporation:** pages 7M, 7R, 30, 31; ©**Brian Kenney:** pages 10T, 17; **Dan Nedrelo:** page 11B; **Photofest:** page 37; **PhotoSpin, Inc.:** page 10B, 13T, 13B, 25; **Allen Blake Sheldon:** pages 1, 3, 6L, 6M, 6R, 7L, 9, 11T, 22, 28; **Rosemary Shelton/Click the Photo Connection:** page 5; **Tom Stack & Associates/Joe McDonald:** page 8.

All of the Internet URLs given in the book were valid at the time of publication. However, due to the dynamic nature of the Internet, some addresses may have changed, or sites may have ceased to exist since publication. While the author and publisher regret any inconvenience this may cause readers, no responsibility for any such changes can be accepted by either the author or the publisher.

Contents

Iguana Introduction

Some people do not think iguanas look like very cuddly pets. Iguanas are active, curious, and very intelligent, and they make great pets. People have loved and even worshiped iguanas for thousands of years. These unique animals remind people of the past, when dinosaurs roamed Earth hundreds of millions of years ago.

Iguanas are very quiet. They make wonderful pets when cared for properly. Iguanas need a great deal of space, light, and heat. They do not need to be walked. Iguanas love to climb. They need rocks, tree branches, and plants in their shelters for climbing. This helps make iguanas feel like they are still living in nature.

An adult should always be in the room when young children are handling an iguana.

■ Iguanas often enjoy spending time with their owners.

Owning a pet iguana is a big responsibility. Owners must spend plenty of time caring for their pet. You will need help from your family to properly care for your iguana. Iguanas need water, food, a warm, safe cage, exercise, and attention to keep them healthy and happy.

Learning what your iguana likes and dislikes will help you take better care of him. Some people think iguanas are unusual pets. Still, if you properly care for your iguana, he can be as friendly and fun as a pet cat or dog.

■ Iguanas are fun and interesting pets for children who are very responsible and have close adult supervision.

Fascinating Facts

- Pet iguanas are either bred on farms or captured in nature. Many people trade iguanas illegally. It is important to buy your iguana from a reputable breeder or pet store.
- There are about 2.25 million pet iguanas in the world.
- Iguanas are sometimes called "herps" because the study of **reptiles** and **amphibians** is called "herpetology." Herpetology comes from the Greek word *herpeton*, which means "things that creep and crawl."

Pet Profiles

Iguanas are lizards. They come in many different shapes, sizes, and colors. There are more than 700 different species of iguanas in the world. Most iguana species do not make good pets. Green iguanas, called *iguana iguanas*, are most commonly kept as pets.

GREEN IGUANA

- Also called the common iguana because it is the best-known species
- Grows to about 6 feet (1.83 meters) long
- Weighs about 20 pounds (9.1 kilograms)
- Lives in South America, Central America, Mexico, the Caribbean, and parts of the United States, including Florida

RHINOCEROS IGUANA

- Has hard, gray skin with three horns on its snout
- Also called rock iguanas because their skin blends in with the rocky coasts of the **Caribbean** islands where they live
- Calm **temperament**
- Easily trained
- Grows between 2 and 4 feet (61 centimeters and 1.22 meters) long

FIJI BANDED IGUANA

- Grows to about 2 feet (61 cm) long
- Enjoys sleeping curled around tall tree branches
- Loves to climb, leap, and swim
- Named for the light-blue stripes that wrap around their green bodies
- Makes a good pet for very experienced owners

Iguanas are part of a group called *iguanids*. Iguanas in the *iguanid* family have unique markings, colors, and features that help the iguanas blend into the area in which they live. Desert iguanas are small and brown so they can blend in with the sand in the Arizona, California, and Nevada deserts where they live.

SPINY-TAILED IGUANA

- Named for their spiny tails
- Loves to dig
- Green at birth; brown, gray, or black as adults
- Changes color when threatened
- Very difficult to tame

CHUCKAWALLA

- Moves very quickly
- Brown, olive, or black skin
- Scientific name is *sauromalus obesus* because when they are in danger they puff up their belly and look obese, or fat
- Has very rough skin that can hurt a person's hand
- Very friendly
- Easily tamed

DESERT IGUANA

- Grows to about 14 (36 centimeters) inches long
- Remains active in temperatures as high as 115 degrees Fahrenheit (46° C)
- Loves to sit in the Sun; skin changes color from brown or gray to pale gray or white at the hottest time of the day
- Makes a good pet

Iguana Origins

Iguanas have lived on Earth for millions of years. Iguanas are not direct **descendants** of dinosaurs. Still, scientists once believed iguanas were related to dinosaurs because they looked like the enormous beasts. Scientists disagree about which species are iguanas' **ancestors**. Many believe iguanas developed from a species that lived in the Galapagos Islands four million years ago.

Spiny-tailed iguanas live in tree branches or near stone walls and rocky slopes in Mexico and Central America.

The name "iguana" comes from the Arawak word *iwana*. The Arawak were the early inhabitants of the Caribbean islands. Christopher Columbus, an explorer who discovered North America, Central America, and South America, traveled to the Caribbean in the 1400s. He renamed the animals "iguanas."

People ate iguanas prior to the 1900s. Like cows, pigs, or sheep, people raised iguanas for food. Iguanas became popular pets in the 1950s. During this time, more people became interested in keeping these exotic, or strange, animals as pets.

Never cool off an iguana by placing it in cold water. Use a spray bottle to mist the iguana or place a damp wash cloth on the animal.

Fascinating Facts

- It is illegal to own an iguana in Hawaii.
- In 1825, a scientist named Gideon Mantell found a dinosaur fossil. He named the dinosaur "iguanadon" because its tooth looked like that of a modern-day iguana.
- Pet stores sold iguanas as "Chinese Dragons" in the 1950s. However, the lizards they sold were not from China.

Life Cycle

Baby and adult iguanas need a great deal of care and attention. Iguanas depend on their owners for food, water, shelter, and health care needs. From a newborn iguana to a mature iguana, your pet's needs will change during her lifetime.

Newborn Iguanas

Iguanas are reptiles. Most reptiles do not give birth to live young. These reptiles lay eggs instead. Female iguanas dig in sand or soil for a place to lay their eggs. Iguanas lay between 12 and 60 eggs at one time. Most iguana eggs must be incubated for 90 to 120 days, depending on the species and temperature. Female iguanas protect the eggs from **predators**. The female leaves once the babies have hatched.

Two Years

Iguanas are fully grown between 2 and 3 years of age. Adult iguanas are not as active as young iguanas. Adult iguanas need less food. They only need to be fed every second day. Adult iguanas still need plenty of exercise. Owners should make sure their iguana's cage is always equipped with branches for their lizard to climb.

Hatchlings

Iguana hatchlings break out of their shells using a **hatch tooth**. The hatch tooth grows on their snout. Iguana hatchlings can see and crawl. They must find their own food and water. Iguana hatchlings grow very quickly. They need to be fed once a day.

Three to Five Months

By 3 months old, iguanas are very active. This is the best time to bring home a pet iguana. They are easily trained and can learn to listen to their new owner.

Fascinating Facts

- Pet iguanas have laid eggs in some strange places, such as in a bed, on the keyboard of a computer, or under a refrigerator.
- Some iguana species are **endangered**. In many countries, they are protected by law.
- Most baby iguanas are about 7 inches (18 cm) long.

Picking Your Pet

There are many factors to consider and research before choosing a pet. Considering these factors will help you select the right pet to bring home. There are some important questions to think about before picking your pet.

What Will an Iguana Cost?

Green iguanas are the most common type of iguana sold in pet stores and by breeders. They are inexpensive to buy. Still, keeping a pet iguana is very costly. Iguanas have many special needs. When calculating the cost of keeping an iguana, be sure to include the cost of food, the cage, a light, heating pads, greenery, branches, and rocks to fill the cage.

Before buying a baby iguana, watch him in his cage. Do not choose an iguana that runs away when being picked up.

■ Iguanas need large shelters. Some owners build their iguana's shelter.

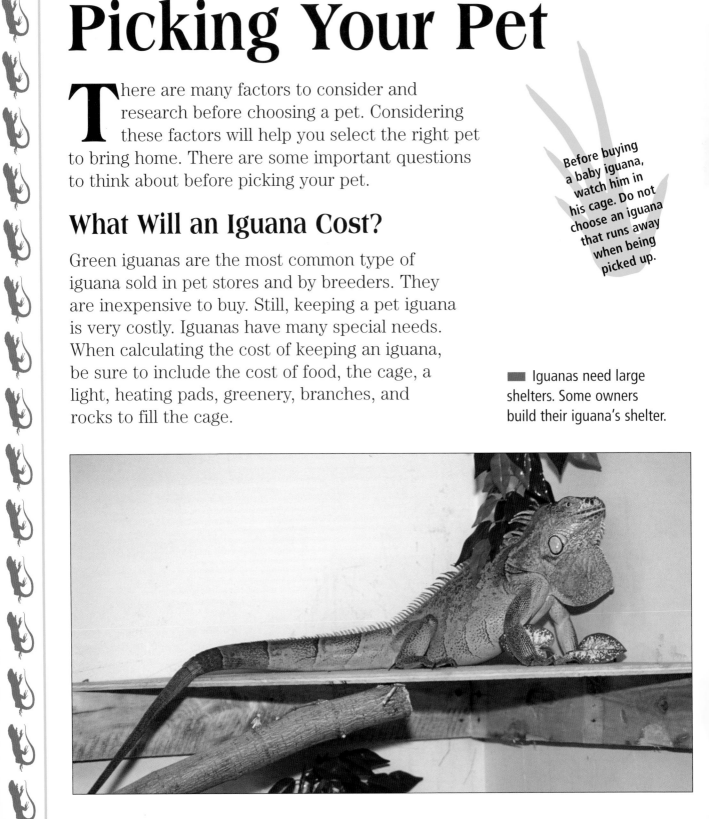

Do I Have Time for an Iguana?

Do you have time to dedicate to your scaly friend every day? It takes a large amount of time and energy to care for an iguana. Iguanas need to be cleaned, fed, **groomed**, and played with every day.

How Will an Iguana Affect My Family?

Before buying an iguana, you must make sure that your parents and siblings are willing to help you take care of your pet. Owning an iguana is a big responsibility. Owners must care for their pet by feeding their iguana and giving it attention. Iguanas also need their cages cleaned often. They need to be bathed and groomed, too. Iguanas can grow very large. This may frighten some family members. Some iguanas do not get along well with other pets, such as cats and dogs.

Iguanas can live to be 15 years or older.

Fascinating Facts

- Birds of prey, foxes, rats, snakes, and weasels eat iguanas. Many animals eat iguana eggs, too.
- In warm places, people often keep their iguanas outside year-round.

Iguana Items

Before bringing an iguana home, make sure you have all the supplies your pet needs to be comfortable in his new environment. Iguanas need to live in large cages or aquariums, called enclosures. They require plenty of space to climb and bask, or lie in a warm place. If you select a baby iguana, you will need to buy new, larger enclosures as the iguana grows. Ask a **veterinarian**, breeder, or a pet store employee what size enclosure is best for your pet iguana.

Iguanas must be housed in a secure enclosure so they cannot escape or be attacked by other animals.

Iguanas need heat and light throughout the day and night to stay healthy. An iguana's enclosure should have special light bulbs that give the iguana the vitamins and heat it needs to survive. Iguanas need humidity, too. Special **humidifiers** can be bought at any pet store. Placing a humidifier in the enclosure will ensure the iguana has enough moisture.

An iguana's enclosure is not complete without decorations. Use linoleum, paper towel, or artificial grass to line the enclosure floor. Place thick tree branches or trees, and rocks inside the enclosure. The iguana will climb and rest on these items. Iguanas also require plants and flowers where they can hide and play.

Heated rocks may hurt your iguana. Since iguanas cannot feel heat, they may lay too close to a heated rock and become burned.

■ Iguanas use the heat from special lamps to help digest their food.

Fascinating Facts

- Iguanas are cold-blooded. This means their bodies do not create their own heat. Iguanas warm up by sitting in the Sun. They cool off by dipping in water.
- Iguanas need to be in sunlight or artificial light for 8 to 12 hours each day.

Iguana Edibles

Iguanas are herbivores. This means they are plant-eating animals. Iguanas will eat most plant foods. Still, iguanas require a very balanced diet that includes a combination of store-bought food, fresh fruits, and vegetables. A pet iguana's diet should include a mixture of dark green, leafy vegetables. Store-bought food should only make up about half of an iguana's diet. Iguanas also eat dandelions, rose petals, carnations, clover, and other flowers. Fresh fruits, such as bananas, berries, apples, and peaches, should only be fed to an iguana as a special treat. Some iguanas may need to have vitamins added to their meals. Vitamins can be purchased at a pet store.

Spinach, parsley, and kale are high in protein. Too much protein causes kidney failure in iguanas.

■ Iguanas should not eat animal meat. It contains large amounts of fats that are not healthy for the iguana.

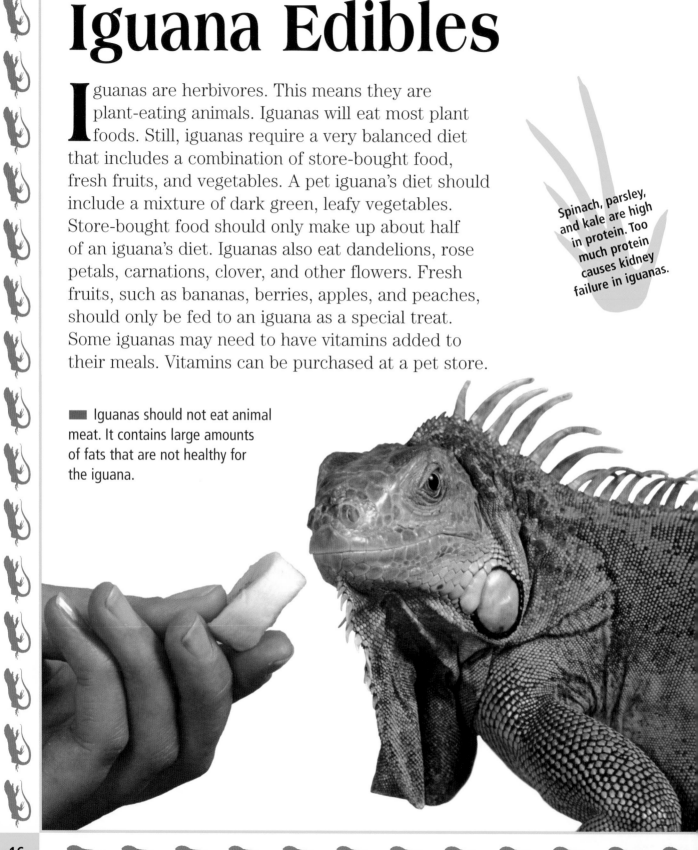

Iguanas are folivores. This means they mostly eat leaves in their natural environment.

How Much Food Should I Give My Iguana?

How much your iguana eats depends on the size and species. Food purchased at pet stores includes feeding instructions. Books can tell you which foods are good and bad for an iguana, too. Most adult iguanas need to eat two or three times each week. Iguanas do not chew their food, so be sure to cut food into small pieces. Soak dry food in water to soften it.

It is important that you talk to a veterinarian to learn about the foods and vitamins your iguana needs. Watch what foods your iguana enjoys eating. If your iguana will not eat certain foods, you can try different combinations of vegetables, plants, and store-bought foods.

Fascinating Facts

- When iguanas are sick, they stop eating. Iguanas that do not eat should be taken to a veterinarian immediately.
- Iguanas should not eat lettuce. Lettuce is like junk food for iguanas. It has very few of the vitamins iguanas need to stay healthy.
- In South and Central America, iguanas are considered a **delicacy**. People in this region often call iguanas *pollo de los arboles*. This means "chicken of the trees." Iguanas live in trees, and they taste like chicken when they are cooked.

Slinky and Spiky

Whether an iguana is large or small, wild or **domesticated**, all iguanas have some common features. All lizards have long tails that help them keep their balance. They also have scales that help protect them from injuries.

▬ **GREEN IGUANA**

Iguanas use their long tails to help keep their balance. Some iguanas have tails that are three times longer than their bodies. Iguanas use their tails for defense, too. An iguana's tail breaks off when a predator grabs it. This allows the iguana to escape from the predator. This does not hurt the iguana. The tail grows back.

Iguanas have powerful back legs that they use to run, swim, and climb.

Iguanas use their toes and sharp claws to hold on to things. In nature, iguanas use their feet to climb trees.

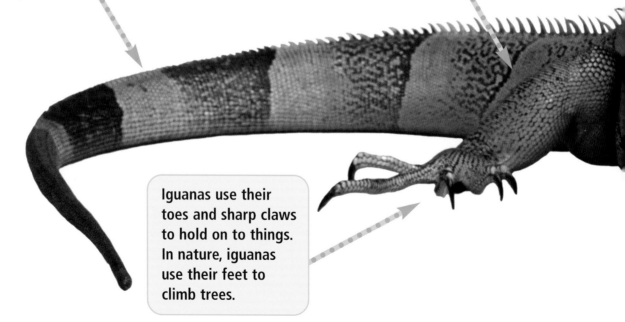

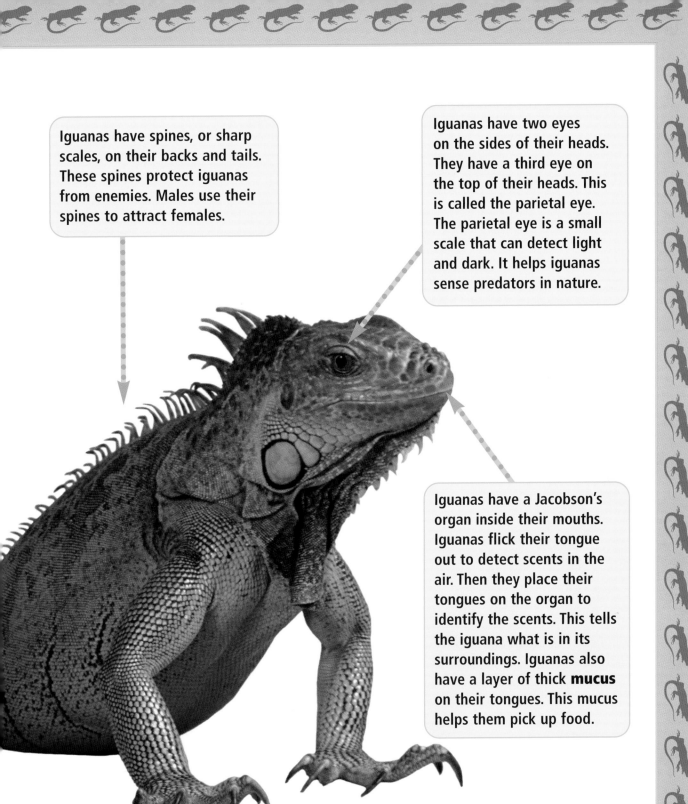

Iguanas have spines, or sharp scales, on their backs and tails. These spines protect iguanas from enemies. Males use their spines to attract females.

Iguanas have two eyes on the sides of their heads. They have a third eye on the top of their heads. This is called the parietal eye. The parietal eye is a small scale that can detect light and dark. It helps iguanas sense predators in nature.

Iguanas have a Jacobson's organ inside their mouths. Iguanas flick their tongue out to detect scents in the air. Then they place their tongues on the organ to identify the scents. This tells the iguana what is in its surroundings. Iguanas also have a layer of thick **mucus** on their tongues. This mucus helps them pick up food.

Reptile Rinse

Iguanas do not groom, or clean, themselves. Iguana owners need to spend time grooming their pet and cleaning her enclosure. Keeping your iguana and her house clean will keep her healthy and happy.

Waste should be removed from the iguana's cage every day. Iguanas need fresh water every day, too. Food and water dishes should be cleaned often. The enclosure and its decorations should be thoroughly washed and disinfected once each week. Use gentle cleansers that will not harm your pet. Be sure to rinse the enclosure and the decorations well.

Iguanas do not enjoy being bathed. Wear gloves when bathing an iguana to avoid being scratched.

■ Mist an iguana and its environment daily to help keep them moist.

Iguanas should be bathed often. Some iguana owners bathe their pets every day. To bathe an iguana, fill the bathtub with water that is chest-deep on the iguana. It is important to make sure the water is not too cold. Use a thermometer to check that the temperature stays between 84.2 and 89.6 degrees Fahrenheit (29° and 32° C). Bathing and misting an iguana helps with shedding, too.

Sometimes, dirt builds up on iguanas. Gently scrubbing the dirty area with a washcloth will remove the dirt. Never use human soap or shampoo on an iguana. Soap and shampoo can harm their eyes, skin, and mouths.

Iguanas should soak in water for about 20 to 30 minutes.

Fascinating Facts

- Iguanas can hold their breath under water for up to 30 minutes.
- Iguanas need to have their claws clipped so they do not get too long. Veterinarians can clip iguana claws. Owners can do it at home with an adult's help.
- Some people think that when iguanas sneeze they have a cold. In fact, iguanas sneeze to clean out glands they have in their noses.
- Iguanas shed their skin. Never pick or peel an iguana's skin.

Healthy and Happy

Keeping an iguana healthy and happy is a big responsibility. Making sure your iguana and its enclosure are clean will help keep your pet healthy. Placing plenty of fresh water inside the enclosure and bathing the iguana daily will help keep the animal healthy, too. Playing with your iguana and making sure she has a large enough space to live, climbing areas, and places to hide will keep her happy.

It is important to find a veterinarian who has experience with iguanas. A good veterinarian will answer any questions you have about your iguana's behavior. A veterinarian will also help if your iguana becomes ill.

■ If the temperature outside is warm, taking an iguana outside can be fun for both owner and pet.

As you spend more time with your iguana, it will be easier for you to notice changes in her personality. Is the iguana avoiding human contact? Is she eating more or less? Are there any changes in the color or texture of the iguana's skin and scales? These things are just some of the signs that the iguana may need veterinary care.

Some veterinarians believe it is safe to let an iguana roam free around the house. If you decide to let your iguana roam free, be sure there is nothing that can hurt her. This includes other animals, such as cats and dogs, that can bite or scratch the iguana. Instead, it is safer to give the iguana a large enclosure where it can play.

Some iguanas do not like wearing a leash and collar. Do not force an iguana to walk on a leash or she may become injured.

Fascinating Facts

- If your iguana escapes, look for her tail. Iguanas love to hide, but they often leave their tails hanging out from their hiding places.
- **Salmonella** is a **virus** that can make humans very sick. Some iguanas carry the bacteria that causes this virus. To prevent this illness, it is important to take iguanas for a checkup once each year. Owners must also keep their iguana's enclosure very clean.

■ Some iguanas like being scratched or lightly stroked on their head.

Iguana Behavior

Iguanas are very independent. It may be a long time before a pet iguana becomes comfortable with his new owner and home. Iguanas do not play with toys like cats or dogs do. It is difficult to train an iguana to sit quietly on your lap. Still, iguana owners can have plenty of fun with their pets.

Iguanas should not be put outdoors in temperatures cooler than 70° F (21° C).

It can take between 6 months and 1 year to tame a pet iguana.

Pet Peeves

Iguanas do not like:
- loud noises
- too much protein
- being too hot or too cold
- being handled often
- dirty water

Iguanas are intelligent. Some can be trained to respond when their name is called. Others may learn when it is time for a meal or a bath. Some iguanas will come to their owners and give their pant leg a tug if they want to climb up.

People and their iguanas cannot communicate through words. It is important to pay attention to your pet's behavior. This will help you know if he is happy, upset, or afraid. Iguanas can be dangerous if they are frightened or angered. They have sharp teeth and spines on their tails, so it is important to stay away if they are upset.

Female iguanas do not grow as large as males. Females are usually more tame, too.

Fascinating Facts

- Domesticated iguanas can spend hours resting wrapped around their owner's neck.
- In New York City, an iguana saved a man's life. The man had a heart attack. His iguana knocked the phone off the hook and stepped on the buttons to call 911.

Iguana Tales

People have feared iguanas throughout history. Iguanas are often portrayed as evil and cruel creatures in **myths** and stories. Still, iguanas are honored and loved in some cultures.

Archaeologists have found carvings of iguanas in Mayan tombs. Mayans were an ancient people who lived in Central America. Mayans worshiped animals. The Mayans believed iguanas were guides that would lead people to their next life after they died. The Pueblo peoples from the southwestern United States also worshiped the lizards. Iguanas are often the subject of Pueblo peoples' art. Stories were told about iguanas in Australia, too. There, ancient peoples told stories of **mischievous** iguana twins who traveled across the desert, creating animals, humans, and plants with their sweeping tails.

Iguanas need about 12 hours of time away from the Sun or artificial light.

Fascinating Facts

- Charles Darwin, who wrote *The Origin of Species*, studied iguanas living on the Galapagos Islands. Darwin was the first person to discover marine iguanas living on the islands. These swimming iguanas are the only living marine lizards.

Iguanas have starred in many popular films and television programs. In the 1950s film *King Dinosaur*, claws and spikes were attached to live iguanas to make them look more like dinosaurs. Authors have written books about iguanas, too. *The Iguana Brothers: A Tale of Two Lizards*, by Tony Johnston and Mark Teague, is a popular children's book.

■ In 1955's *King Dinosaur*, four people travel to a planet that is home to a giant iguana.

This book is about the adventures of two iguana brothers named Tom and Dom who live in Mexico. The book is being produced as a feature-length cartoon.

The Mosquito and the Iguana

A traditional African folktale explains why mosquitoes buzz. Once upon a time, mosquitoes could talk. In fact, mosquitoes talked all the time. One day, mosquito was telling iguana a story about a recent trip. He told iguana every detail of the trip, from what he packed to what he ate, and where he traveled to what he bought. Iguana was not able to say a single word because mosquito talked without stopping. Iguana became upset with mosquito. Mosquito kept talking as iguana walked away. Mosquito was so annoyed she walked right past snake. This made snake sad. Snake decided to hide inside a rabbit hole. This frightened rabbit, who ran from the hole. Crow saw rabbit running and began to caw as a warning to the other animals. Monkey heard the warning. He began jumping from one tree branch to another. One branch broke and an owl's nest fell to the ground. The eggs inside the nest broke. This made owl sad. She was so sad that she did not hoot for the Sun to rise. All the animals grew angry with mosquito. Then, owl hooted for the Sun to rise. Mosquito lost his voice as it rose. Now, "zzzzz" was the only sound mosquito could make.

Pet Puzzlers

What do you know about iguanas? If you can answer the following questions correctly, you may be ready to own a pet iguana.

Q Do iguanas groom themselves?

No, iguanas do not groom themselves. It is important for iguana owners to bathe and clean their iguanas often.

Q What does an iguana's parietal eye do?

The parietal eye helps iguanas detect light and dark. It also helps iguanas sense danger.

Q What does an iguana need inside her enclosure?

Iguanas need a large amount of space, a plastic or artificial grass floor, branches, rocks, plants, a light, heater, and humidifier.

Q How often should you take your iguana for a checkup?

Iguanas need to see a veterinarian at least once each year.

Q When did iguanas become popular pets?

Iguanas did not become popular pets until the 1950s.

Q What can iguanas be trained to do?

Many iguanas can learn to respond when their names are called or know when it is time to have a meal or a bath. Some can even be trained to sit on their owner's laps or shoulders.

Q What food should your iguana never eat?

Iguanas should never eat junk food such as lettuce. Ask a veterinarian which foods are healthy for your iguana.

Iguana Icons

Before you buy your pet iguana, write down some iguana names that you like. Some names may work better for a female iguana. Others may suit a male iguana. Here are a few suggestions:

Iggy

Iguardo

Rocky

Hissy

Dino Jr.

Tom

Dom

Spike

Speedy

Curly

Frequently Asked Questions

Should I buy a male or female iguana?

The main difference between male and female iguanas is their size. Most male iguanas grow about 2 feet (61 cm) longer than female iguanas. Male iguanas may be more aggressive than females. **Neutering** male iguanas helps make them less aggressive.

Which vitamins should I give my iguana?

Depending on the species and age of your iguana, you will need to give him supplements, or vitamins. Some iguanas do not get enough vitamin D in their regular diets. Pet stores sell vitamins in liquid or tablet form. Supplements may also contain a combination of vitamins A, C, and E.

Are iguanas bad pets for young children?

Some veterinarians and breeders believe that iguanas do not make good pets for very young children. This is because they require a great deal of care. Iguanas are often loving, affectionate, and can be tamed. The main factors to consider before buying a pet iguana is their large size, and the length of time it takes to groom, clean, and feed these animals. With an adult's help, an iguana can make a wonderful pet for a young child.

More Information

Animal Organizations

You can help iguanas stay happy and healthy by learning more about them. Many organizations are dedicated to teaching people how to care for and protect their pet pals. For more iguana information, write to the following organizations:

International Iguana Society
133 Steele Road
West Hartford, CT 06119

Humane Society of the United States
2100 L Street N.W.
Washington, D.C. 20037

Web Sites

To answer more of your iguana questions, go online and surf to the following Web sites:

International Iguana Society
www.iguanasociety.org

Green Iguana Society
www.greenigsociety.org

Melissa Kaplan's Herp Care Collection
www.anapsid.org

Words to Know

amphibians: animals that live both on land and in water

ancestors: animals from the past that are related to modern animals

archaeologists: scientists who study objects from the past

Caribbean: the name of a region in the Atlantic Ocean

delicacy: something pleasing

descendants: those who follow

domesticated: tamed, not wild

endangered: animals whose populations are so low they are in danger of disappearing completely

groomed: cleaned by removing dirt from skin

hatch tooth: a sharp point on the tip of the jaw that falls off after hatching

humidifiers: devices that create moisture

mischievous: playing in a naughty or teasing way

mucus: a slimy substance produced by the body

myths: ancient stories that explain the history of a group of people

neutering: making male animals unable to reproduce

predators: animals that hunt and kill other animals for food

reptiles: cold-blooded animals with rough, scaly skin

salmonella: a type of bacteria that causes flu-like symptoms that can lead to death

temperament: personality

veterinarian: animal doctor

virus: an illness

Index